CLAWS

AND JAWS

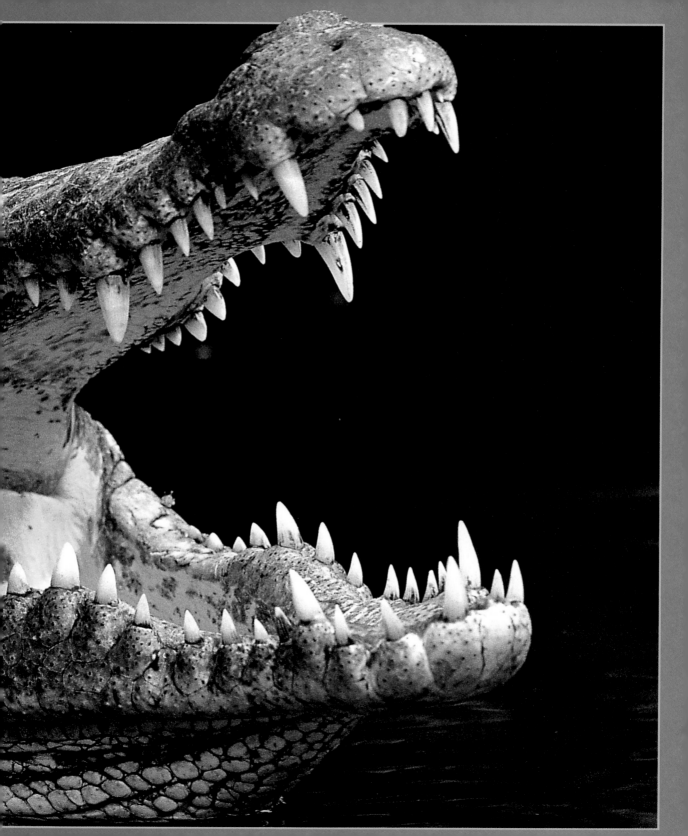

Picture Credits

R.E. Barber: pages 15, 24-25, 28
Bill Beatty: page 29
Cathy & Gordon Illg: page 9
Gary Kramer: page 14
Dwight Kuhn: page 10
Tom & Pat Leeson: pages 8, 24
Robert & Linda Mitchell: pages 6, 19
Norbert Wu: Cover; page 22
Denis Paquin/AP Photo: page 16
Tom Brakefield/DRK: pages 6-7, 18-19, 22-23
Chamberlain, M.C./DRK: page 27
Marty Cordano/DRK: page 12
Chuck Dresner/DRK: page 25
Michael Fogden/DRK: pages 7, 11, 25
Stephen J. Krassemen/DRK: page 18
Dwight Kuhn/DRK: page 28
C.C. Lockwood/DRK: page 26
S. Nielson/DRK: page 21
Doug Perrine/DRK: page 9
Leonard Lee Rue III/DRK: pages 20-21
Anup Shah/DRK: Endpages; page 23
Jeremy Woodhouse/DRK: page 20
Norbert Wu/DRK: page 26
George Grall/National Geographic Society: page 29
Robert F. Sisson/National Geographic Society: page 13
A.J. Copley/Visuals Unlimited: page 11
Dave B. Fleetham/Visuals Unlimited: page 23
A. Kerstitch/Visuals Unlimited: pages 26-27
Ken Lucas/Visuals Unlimited: page 17
Joe McDonald/Visuals Unlimited: page 10
Glenn M. Oliver/Visuals Unlimited: pages 14-15
Science VU/Visuals Unlimited: page 14
Stephen Frink/Waterhouse: page 12
HPH Photography/The Wildlife Collection: pages 12-13
Chris Huss/The Wildlife Collection: page 19
Tom Vezo/The Wildlife Collection: pages 9, 21

Illustrations:
Howard S. Friedman: page 16

Published by Rourke Publishing LLC

Copyright © 2002 Kidsbooks, Inc.

Printed in the USA

Grambo, Rebecca
  Claws and Jaws / Rebecca L. Grambo
    p. cm – (Amazing Animals)
    ISBN 1-58952-142-0

CLAWS
AND JAWS

Written By

Rebecca L. Grambo

Rourke Publishing LLC
Vero Beach, Florida 32964
rourkepublishing.com

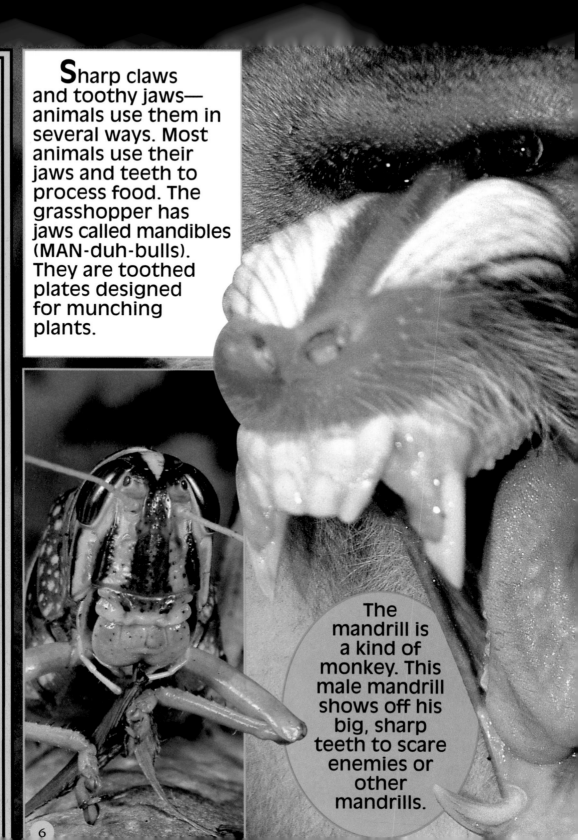

Sharp claws and toothy jaws— animals use them in several ways. Most animals use their jaws and teeth to process food. The grasshopper has jaws called mandibles (MAN-duh-bulls). They are toothed plates designed for munching plants.

The mandrill is a kind of monkey. This male mandrill shows off his big, sharp teeth to scare enemies or other mandrills.

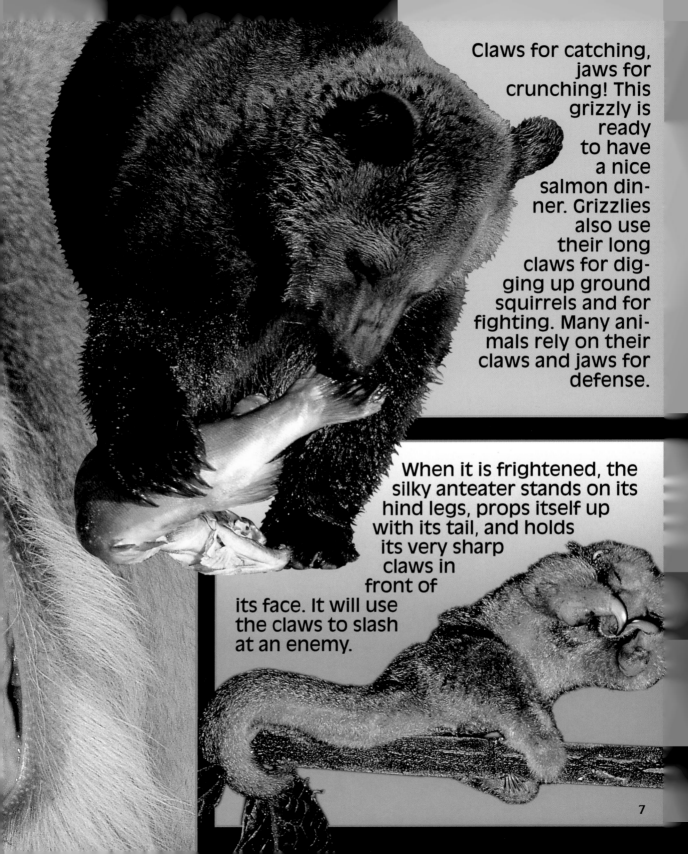

Claws for catching, jaws for crunching! This grizzly is ready to have a nice salmon dinner. Grizzlies also use their long claws for digging up ground squirrels and for fighting. Many animals rely on their claws and jaws for defense.

When it is frightened, the silky anteater stands on its hind legs, props itself up with its tail, and holds its very sharp claws in front of its face. It will use the claws to slash at an enemy.

YOU ARE WHAT YOU EAT!

An animal's jaws and teeth are built for a specialized diet. Animals that hunt other animals are called carnivores (CAR-nuh-vorz). Carnivores need sharp, strong teeth to catch and kill their prey. The long, pointed fangs in this wolf's mouth are called canines (KAY-nines). Most carnivores have big canines.

The upper jaws of certain kinds of whales have big plates of a bristly material called baleen (buh-LEEN). The whales feed by taking a big gulp of water, then forcing the water out through the baleen. The bristles trap even the tiniest food, which the whale swallows. Baleen whales can eat as much as two and a half tons a day!

Deer have no front teeth on top, and the ones on the bottom are quite small. A deer uses the big flat teeth along the sides of its jaws to grind up the plant food that it eats.

Rodents like this coypu (KOY-poo) have long front teeth called incisors (in-SIGH-zurs). The incisors never stop growing. Because rodents chew a lot, their incisors stay very sharp. That means rodents can eat hard foods, such as nuts and seeds.

FANGS-A-LOT

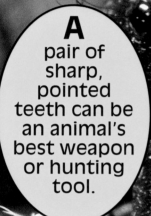

A pair of sharp, pointed teeth can be an animal's best weapon or hunting tool.

As the jumping spider leaps, its jaws open wide and huge fangs unfold from each end. When the spider lands on its prey, it is ready to bite.

A snake's fangs fold up against the roof of its mouth until needed. They work like a hollow needle, injecting poison into prey. Some snakes have fangs nearly two inches long!

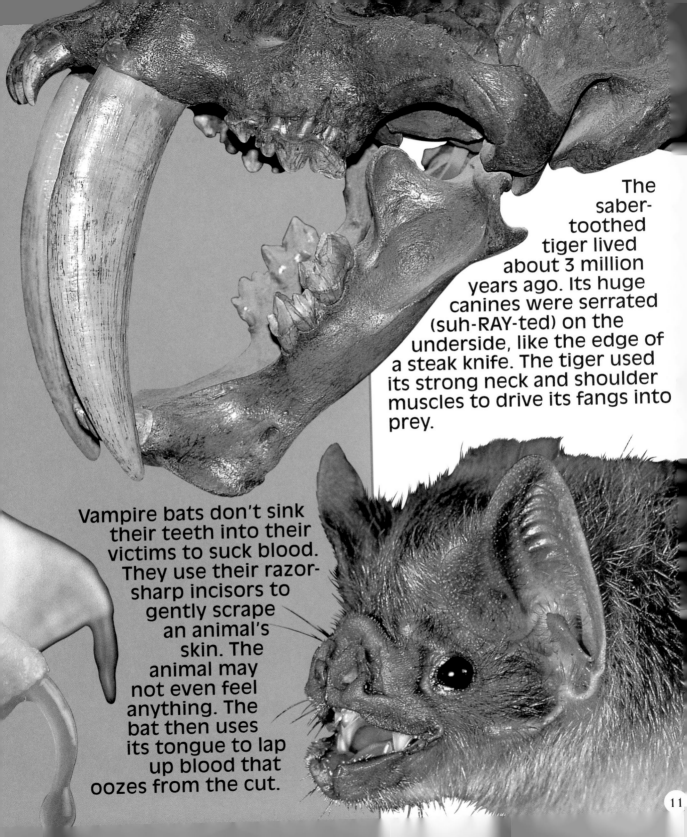

The saber-toothed tiger lived about 3 million years ago. Its huge canines were serrated (suh-RAY-ted) on the underside, like the edge of a steak knife. The tiger used its strong neck and shoulder muscles to drive its fangs into prey.

Vampire bats don't sink their teeth into their victims to suck blood. They use their razor-sharp incisors to gently scrape an animal's skin. The animal may not even feel anything. The bat then uses its tongue to lap up blood that oozes from the cut.

11

MORE THAN CLAWS

Sometimes claws have added features for helping animals catch or eat food.

The scorpion has tiny hairs on its claws that sense movement in the air. Then the scorpion grabs and stings its victim.

Underneath the horseshoe crab is a mass of legs. The legs end in claws that work like jaws, catching clams and worms. Then these "claw jaws" grind up the food before the horseshoe takes a mouthful.

The five-inch-long mantis shrimp is armed and dangerous. Its claws fold up like knife blades. But it can snap them out in a flash to spear or club its food. Sometimes it even attacks other mantis shrimps.

Waving its oversized claw in the air, a male fiddler crab signals to females nearby. It also uses the big claw to defend its home. The really important job of gathering up food is done by the crab's small claw.

TUSK TUSK TUSK!

Some teeth called tusks are very, very long! The narwhal (NAR-wall) is a whale that lives in northern oceans. Male narwhals have a single ivory tusk that can grow to be almost 10 feet long.

Both the upper and lower canines of a warthog grow up and out to form tusks. Warthogs are plant-eaters. They would rather run than fight. But when they have to fight, they use their tusks to defend themselves.

The canine teeth of a walrus grow into tusks that may be almost three feet long. The walrus uses its tusks for digging up shellfish and to help pull itself onto shore. Walruses also use their tusks when they fight.

14

Both male and female African elephants grow tusks. These big front teeth can be over 11 feet long and weigh more than 200 pounds each, but most are smaller. The big tusks aren't as important to the elephant as its smaller, grinding teeth. It needs those teeth to eat properly.

DINO MIGHT!

Dinosaurs had bigger claws and jaws than those of any animal living today. Carcharodontosaurus (KAR-kar-uh-DON-toh-SORE-us) had eight-inch teeth in its six-foot-long head.

Tyrannosaurus (tuh-RAN-uh-SORE-us) was built for eating meat. Designed for biting and tearing flesh, the teeth in this dino's four-foot skull were about six inches long and sharp as knives.

16

Deinonychus (die-NON-ick-us) was only about four feet tall. But it had a huge five-inch claw on its second toe. When Deinonychus ran, the claw folded up to stay out of the way. The claw moved into position for kicking and slashing when Deinonychus attacked its prey.

DIG THIS

Some animals have claws made for digging and shoveling.

The badger's strong legs end in big claws, which are used to dig up small animals to eat. A badger can dig faster in loose dirt than a person can with a shovel.

18

Moles have paddle-shaped front paws that end in sharp claws. They have ridges on their front toes that help them move dirt. Moles dig by "swimming" through the dirt, first using one paw, then the other.

The mole cricket lives like a mole. The cricket's sharp claws and bristles on its legs help it move through the soil.

Giant anteaters use their two long, sharp, curved claws to rip into termite mounds. The mounds may be as hard as concrete, but that doesn't stop the anteater.

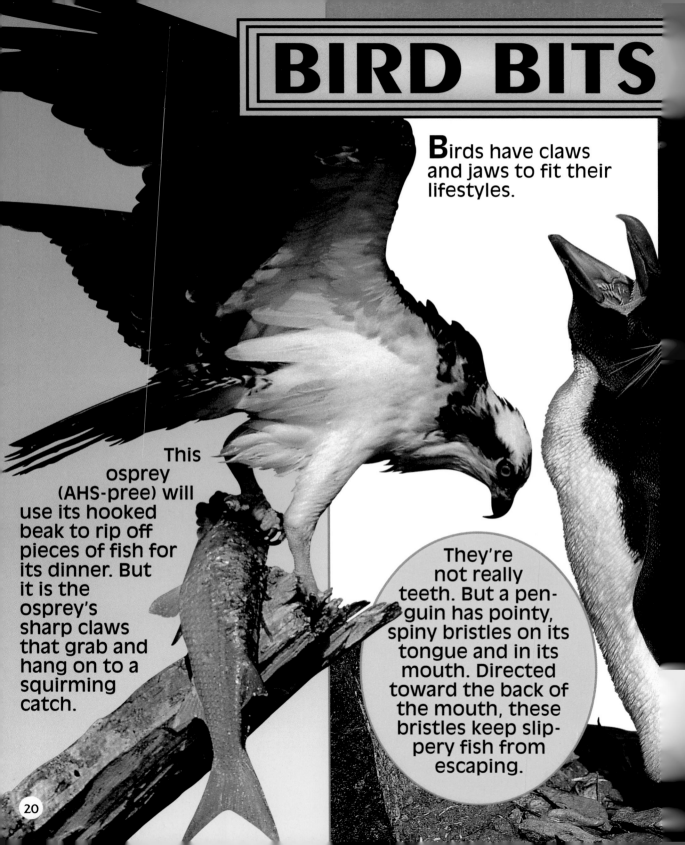

BIRD BITS

Birds have claws and jaws to fit their lifestyles.

This osprey (AHS-pree) will use its hooked beak to rip off pieces of fish for its dinner. But it is the osprey's sharp claws that grab and hang on to a squirming catch.

They're not really teeth. But a penguin has pointy, spiny bristles on its tongue and in its mouth. Directed toward the back of the mouth, these bristles keep slippery fish from escaping.

Woodpecker feet have two toes facing forward, and two pointing to the back. Along with its stiff tail, its toes help the woodpecker balance safely on the side of trees. Then the bird can use its strong bill to poke around in the bark for insects.

Herons eat fish. To catch them, the heron stabs the fish with its sharp bill, which sometimes goes right through the fish. Herons also have a special, flattened claw on one of their toes. They use it for combing through their feathers.

SCARY JAWS

The great white shark's mouth is full of sharp teeth. Like other sharks, its teeth grow in rows, one row behind the other. The teeth aren't hooked to the shark's jaw, but grow out of the skin. When the teeth in the first row wear out, they drop out. The teeth behind them move forward. Over ten years' time, a shark may go through more than 20,000 teeth.

Some animals have a mouth that looks frightening, but these scary jaws do important jobs for the animals.

A roaring lion gives us a good look at his teeth. Hunting cats like lions have very large, sharp canines. Lions use both their claws and jaws to capture and kill their food.

Crocodiles don't have lips, their teeth show, and their mouth leaks even when closed. Even with all those teeth, crocodiles can't chew. They just gulp their food down in big chunks. But those big jaws are very good for grabbing prey.

Moray eels have long, thin teeth designed for catching and holding small prey. Their biggest teeth are hinged, folding back to make it easier for the eels' lunch to slide on by.

GET A GRIP

Claws help animals to catch food, grip tree limbs, and defend themselves.

Animals that spend some or all of their time in trees need their claws to keep them from falling. Babies like this raccoon learn right away how to hang on.

Just like a house cat, the mountain lion keeps its claws tucked in so they stay sharp. When it wants to fight, climb, or catch prey, the big cat extends its claws. This mountain lion is sharpening its claws on a tree.

Without its claws, the sloth wouldn't be able to hang around. It spends its life climbing or hanging upside down, with its strong claws hooked over branches. The sloth also uses its claws to pull off leaves to eat.

Bird legs are designed so that the toes tighten around a perch when the bird lands. That's why birds don't fall off their branches when they sleep.

INCREDIBLE JAWS

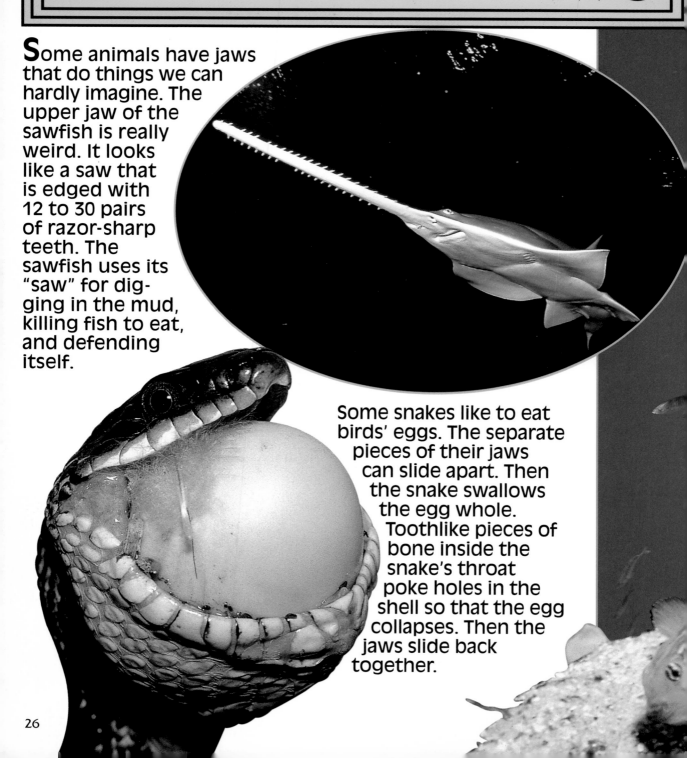

Some animals have jaws that do things we can hardly imagine. The upper jaw of the sawfish is really weird. It looks like a saw that is edged with 12 to 30 pairs of razor-sharp teeth. The sawfish uses its "saw" for digging in the mud, killing fish to eat, and defending itself.

Some snakes like to eat birds' eggs. The separate pieces of their jaws can slide apart. Then the snake swallows the egg whole. Toothlike pieces of bone inside the snake's throat poke holes in the shell so that the egg collapses. Then the jaws slide back together.

The jaws of a whale shark have thousands of teeth and are wide enough to swallow two people. But don't worry. The whale shark eats only small fish and shrimp—lots of them! Its teeth are tiny—much smaller than yours.

The cone shell does its hunting with only one tooth. The tooth may be almost half an inch long. It is thin and hollow. The cone shell fires the tooth into its prey like a harpoon. Then the cone shell's strong poison paralyzes the prey.

BUG BITES

In the insect world, claws and jaws come in strange shapes. The "horns" on this male stag beetle are really just overgrown jaws. The beetle uses them for attracting a mate or for fighting with other males, but not for eating.

Dragonflies live underwater for a while before they grow wings. Young dragonflies are called nymphs (NIMFS). Nymphs have jaws that fold up over their face like a mask. They can unfold them quickly to catch prey.

This trap-jaw ant has very sensitive hairs along its jaws. If the hairs feel prey, the ant's jaws close like a trap. The pointy tips of the jaw stab the prey and hold it while the ant stings it.

Mantids have lots of spines and hooks on their front legs. They hunt by ambush, waiting for prey to get too close. Then those big front legs snap together!